From

Panographs® by Ken Duncan

Introduction

Worry and fear have no nationality and affect people all over the world. I have seen many ways of trying to deal with them. The following pages provide the key which allows us to look beyond our present circumstances and to hope in something far greater than ourselves. As you reflect upon the beauty of God's creation in these photographs, may the accompanying words penetrate your heart and bring you hope.

Ken Duncan.

Don't worry about your Life

Don't worry about
having something
to Eat

Don't worry about
having something
to Drink

Don't worry about having something to *Wear*

Isn't life more
than Food
or clothing?

Look at the Birds

in the sky!

The birds don't plant or *Harvest*

The birds

don't even store Grain

in barns

Yet your Father
in Heaven
takes care of them

Aren't you
Worth more than
birds?

Don't worry
and ask yourselves,
"Will we have
anything to eat,
drink or wear?"

Only people who
Don't know God
are always worrying
about such things

Your Father in heaven

knows that you need

All of these

But more than
anything else ...

Put God's work
First and do
what he wants

Then the
other things *W*ill be
yours as well

Don't worry about your life.
Don't worry about having something to eat.
Don't worry about having something to drink.
Don't worry about having something to wear.
Isn't life more than food or clothing?

Look at the birds in the sky!
The birds don't plant or harvest.
The birds don't even store grain in barns.
Yet your Father in heaven takes care of them.
Aren't you worth more than birds?

Don't worry and ask yourselves, "Will we have anything to eat, drink or wear?"
Only people who don't know God are always worrying about such things.
Your Father in heaven knows that you need all of these.
But more than anything else, put God's work first and do what he wants.
Then the other things will be yours as well.

Taken from Matthew Chapter 6

PHOTO INDEX

Let There Be Hope

FIRST PUBLISHED IN 1996
THIS EDITION PUBLISHED 1997
REPRINTED 1999
BY KEN DUNCAN PANOGRAPHS® PTY LTD
ACN 050 235 606
PO BOX 3015, WAMBERAL NSW 2260
TELEPHONE: (02) 4367 6777
www.kenduncan.com

ISBN 0 9586681 7 5

DISTRIBUTED BY
THE BIBLE SOCIETY IN AUSTRALIA INC.
30 YORK ROAD, INGLEBURN NSW 2565
PRINTED IN HONG KONG BY SOUTH CHINA PRINTING CO.